Quarry

Cape Breton Quarry

STEWART DONOVAN

Breton Books
Wreck Cove, Cape Breton Island
1994

Copyright © 1994 by Stewart L. Donovan

Poems in *Cape Breton Quarry* have appeared in *The Antigonish Review*, *The Fiddlehead* and *The Nashwaak Review*.

My thanks to Ronald Caplan for his editorial suggestions in helping bring the manuscript of *Cape Breton Quarry* into finished book form. Thanks as well to Bonnie Thompson and Sharon Hope Irwin for their careful reading. And to David Conrad.
    —Stewart Donovan

Cover photograph: Mike MacDougall's crew hauling a mackerel trap off Ingonish, Cape Breton Island.
Photograph: Ronald Caplan; Darkroom Work: Grant Young.

Canadian Cataloguing in Publication Data

    Donovan, Stewart L. (Stewart Leo)

        Cape Breton quarry

        Poems.
        ISBN 1-895415-44-6

    I. Title.

PS8557.0583C37 1994   C811'.54   C94-950256-1
PR9199.3.D66C37 1994

For Ann and Leo

The Poems

Cann's Lake, Ingonish *1*
Saturday Night in Sydney *2*
Cape Breton Quarry *3*
First Charlotte Street Show, 1959 *8*
Sydney-Glace Bay Drive-in *9*
Halifax Report on Sydney Cancer Rates *10*
Down by the Tar Ponds *12*
Cape Breton Journal *13*
Ingonish Inshore *17*
Antigonish Landing *18*
Death of the Inshore *22*
from Ingonish Intervale *25*
Cabot Day *28*
Quebec North of Englishtown *29*
Long Distance: coast to coast *31*
Calgary Breton Blues *32*
Knight Inlet, B.C. *33*
Homemade Stars *35*
Partridge Island, Saint John *36*
General James Wolfe enroute
   from Halifax to Quebec, 1759 *39*
Loyalists Landing at Sydney *40*
The White Buildings on Shea's Hill *42*
A Japanese Western *46*
Bewley's Oriental Café, Dublin *47*
Dublin's McLuhan *48*
Liscomb Sanctuary *49*
Cape Breton Christmas *52*
Post War Mementos *54*

Cann's Lake, Ingonish

A dull thud brought the black cadillac to a halt
Fortunately in front of Doucette's station
(With Peter in) and Grand-uncle Harry out
Of luck even on this day, his last.

Laugh, yes, and swear possibly too, with his
Contempt of 50 years for progress
And the National Park which took his land,
Traps, trails and boyhood.

"Baddeck is a hole," he grumbled to my father,
Recalling the comfort of his Cann's Lake cabin
A shack with no water, no toilet, a woodstove and
Squirrels for company.

All but my mother thought him crazy
"Living in there at his age"
She, too, worried though, and sent my brothers in
As soon as the storm had ended.

Arriving midday cold, hungry and tired,
He fed them sending them home before dusk
With handmade moccasins (his) for my mother
And to her only would he surrender in the spring

Baddeck was beautiful, the lakes below the window and
Bell's museum just down the road
No he would not go, having seen the old inventor with Corson
A hundred times at Middle Head

Stealing apples then in the Yankee's orchard
Almost caught one Saturday his heart stopped
And the final ride along John Cabot's trail
Until, the gas-tank repaired, he entered the Park.

Saturday Night in Sydney

My friend Paddy lives in Sydney
and the other night when he went home
his wife had taken all the curtains down.
Jamming them into the basement sink
between tears and Javex she cried
"Their time has come can you not see that!"
He said he could and went back upstairs
to sit in the plate-glass window furniture
section of Sears, as their home
had become a department store.

A boy of ten he clutched his mother's
sweating palm through the halls of
Sydney River Hospital—"Nut house,"
his father said waiting in the car
for the coffin. His father always regretted
buying the black Ford Falcon wagon.
"I'm a lineman not a goddam undertaker."
But he never refused the coffins of neighbours
or cousins. Paddy's Aunt Rita had survived
the lobotomy, "a great success but for the heart."

At 13 he saw his cousin Monica return
from Montreal
a flower child with a shaven head
and her young white teeth spread wide.

Now, at 35, he prepares to live lonely
on Saturday nights remembering his wife
wrapped in red wet curtains, crying
for Sunlight soap, her husband, and the damned.

Cape Breton Quarry

The backhoe broke headstones so he blistered
His hands on six inches of frozen earth
Until the soft cool clay gave way to granite
Again. "Newfoundland's gift to us," John Doyle
Grinned. A causeway of rock from Money Point
To Port Aux Basques: underwater umbilical cord,
Englishtown ferry cable, an ancestral chunnel
Linking back and deep in challenge to Canso's
Grim emigrant bridge. John Doyle grieved alone

For cousin Dan MacDonald returned home
To fish, not for a living, but for the feel
Of wet rope on a hawler, the jerk of cod
On a handline, fried roe in the fo'c's'le,
Barbados molasses and tea the colour of coffee.
He died at 42. Not at sea like his cousin David,
But in bed: poor diet and genes.
His grandfather Doyle hooking him back
With high cholesterol and Canadian Club.

No maritime life on the west coast
No wife but the Vancouver-Seattle run
And a recognition at low tide that
At some level we are all Americans.
He drove for Irving Oil from Ingonish
To Pleasant Bay. Liquid coal his grandfather
MacLellan had never burned. Not buried beneath
Cape Breton, or buried too deep to touch. Oak Island.
Captain Kidd in the cab of a Ford two ton.

Hibernia, how he justified returning east.
The *Ocean Ranger* a floating Hilton of hope
And quick money from Heart's Desire

To Yellowknife. Cut-backs, recessions, shut-downs:
Death of the offshore, despair in the rigging,
Death on the rig. A *Titanic* with descendant Irish
On the upper deck. First class. The *Alexander
Kieland's* North Atlantic cousin. A Viking burial
Convoy from Avalon to Aberdeen: trial pieces.

A sentimental siren call cursed from Burlington
To Burnaby and back. A call demanding all. Collect.
Inviolate nostalgia out bill-collecting even Christmas.
A sense of place as old as Appalachians, as remote
As childhood. Banks of the Miramichi, the Island, the Rock,
Donegal, Cape Breton, Belfast, Isle of Skye, Palestine....
"Why do Maritimers hunger so much for home?" John Doyle
Demands of his brother. "A land of no hope or glory,"
His brother Bill returns. "A Celtic fate for all"

"If it's not buried any deeper than Dan, it remains
A mystery to me why women and men return to this."
He grimaced in reply, striking his grandfather's stone
And asking, "What has local history made of his bones?
Besides his tandering in the snow and the fact the British
Navy whipped his great grandfather for desertion."
He used tandering as if it were a word borrowed from
The pages of *The Post* or late night news on CBC.
A word he heard his brother use three days before.

A pre-Columbian cloak of Indian survival art;
A Micmac means of finding winter meat; burrow beneath
The snow like Inuit or Dene dogs; to tander:
A non-exportable infinitive of native nights
Under the cold Crab nebula of Capricorn. To hibernate
Till morning, a grotto of shelter in the Highland Barrens.
Moose meat cut and packed, caribou caught in four
Foot drifts made fifteen by frightened steps
Too close to bent spruce, black shafts of bark.

The word his brother mined from village faith
Mined, too, the fortune of Jeremiah Doyle
A sister Selenia recalling thin white lines
On an old man's back. Pressed from a curragh at Bantry
His father cursing a British frigate captain,
Cape Breton bound from Bristol. Escape. Capture.
Flogging. Escape again. Five years in Ingonish until
Marriage in a Placentia Bay parish to Mary of County
Kerry. His Stella Maris he had not seen since seventeen.

John Doyle warmed to this romance: Grimm tales
For childhood, a chance to kick at the British
Cat. Limeys whom his father loved and fought beside
In Flanders. Unable to accept Dieppe for what it was.
Mountbatten still a boy's hero for a Highlander at 66.
Industry or war, First or Second, all mean the same at 17:
Maritime rites of passage past the woods, the mines, the
Grand Banks, mother and father. A Hudson's Bay Mecca
For Orkney Scots. Great Western Harvest Excursion—*in perpetuum*.

The brothers traded pick for spade and bar. Bill Doyle
Blistered in minutes his city hands. John cursed again,
"Might as well be in the goddam mines or cutting tombs
In Kelly's Mountain cliffs." So again, in self-righteous
Anger, he bullied his brother into history, private and
Public, buoyed by whisky and warm muscles and sweat in March.
Time out of time, a day and a day, beyond themselves. Requiem.
Sleet on the line clotting the kitchen clock. A transformer
Down for good. Ash Wednesday snow. The Lenten touch for Dan.

"Do you remember Dan Dunne?" Bill nodded in reply.
Recalling the first time he'd seen his father cry.
They found the old man frozen in February. Hands in banks
Of ice four feet from home. Village giant, sentimental
Drunk. "What a waste!" the Aunt had cried. How he could make
Their mother laugh. Big Dan. How he could fish, alone in the dory,

Boats gathered round, cod to the gunnels, a giant grinning
In forty fathoms. Greek god of the sea, forever salting fish
In Ingonish. Old netting and glass buoys. Captains Courageous.

Purse seining, as old as Portugal, as dead as Poseidon.
Young boys watching, 12 miles east, for Russian factory
Ships. A line of light from Spanish Bay to Broad Cove,
Or so it seemed at thirteen. Big boned Russian women cooking
Borscht between the decks, under the silent stars of the bear.
Blaming and cursing them all: Portuguese, Spanish, Russian
And Basque. Men and boys from Lisbon with a claim to the cod
of Tierra De Los Bretones two hundred years before the British.
Halifax frigates firing across bows of Nantucket boats.

Cape Cod cousins whose grandfathers cursed and blessed
The *Bluenose*. Law of the sea. Law of the jungle!
How has it come to this off George's Bank! Nova Scotia an
Aberration in an Amsterdam court. Big boats and Albertan
Ambition, the uncontrolled catch, the law of the locust.
The death of the crab, Canso and Caraquet. Family planning
For outports and salmon. Smallwood correct in grim
Retrospect. And Ottawa so far from the sea. Ottawa that left
Unprotected a playground where only sea urchins survive.

John Doyle paced off his work eyeing the steeple
Of his grandfather's church. "He painted that at
Seventy-five and I thank God he's not alive to see
The mess they've made." A classic Gothic form that
Stood in black and white for sixty years, metamorphosed
In a month to a Disney castle baby blue with pews
Turned sideways for all to view. Like Pharisees on show
They could not pray and so demanded back the simple
Shell their Publican fathers built.

"The Church is done and in my own time too"
John Doyle grieved aloud for Father Dan McLeod

In Newfoundland: told to take his collar off
By a passerby. No Samaritans need apply.
The Irish Church triumphant. Cursed? The heresy
Of celibacy and of a man they could not correct.
To kick out St. Christopher and leave the rest
Rudderless in an all but empty boat, unblessed.
"It's sad to see it end like this."

The grand-uncles had been priests: at worst a way
Of escape, freedom from the miners' latrines
They'd learned to clean at seventeen; at best a chance
To make a mark, to do some good as Father Coady
Knew they could. Cape Breton Catholics under siege,
Secular, a different way, working in silence, holding Rome
At bay. A communist from the Margaree mud—to some.
But Marx and Newman would have understood, the cost of
Co-ops, the sale of goods. A chance to see your labour's end.

"He loved the blessing of the boats," John Doyle recalls
Sitting on the edge of Parnell Hawley's wharf. The fishermen
A parody of Sunday fashion with wives and children
On stems and gunnels. *In Nomine Patris*...then a frantic
Rush to the harbour's head following the wake of Ambrose
Whitty's new V8. Fresh greens and reds gleaming in the
Spray-whitened sky off Ingonish, White Point, Cheticamp,
Mabou, Gabarus.... All along Cape Breton's coast
A mingling of incense, kelp, water, wine and host.

The job done the brothers brushed away the cool clay.
Departure for Bill. Turbulence at 7, history at 11. Home.
Last week a Mississauga son moved his finger across and
Across a Maritime map, calling out in clear tones that "There
Was no Golden Age...only tourism now." Are these the facts of
Fate? The old bell tolls a final call for Dan. While over the
Stones, on hole number three, children shout "off-side, and no
Fair." The ice so smooth and bright their sharpened Christmas
Skates cut no glass edge on a joyful slide towards the green.

First Charlotte Street Show, 1959

We staggered blind from the Paramount
into Charlotte street, our eyes hurting
in the August heat, even though the sun
seemed cool in contrast to the greenhouse
humidity of Ceylon: tropical celluloid sticking
us to our back row seats. We all walked on
from the River Kwai, in silence, to the cool
pools of Centennial Park where the smell
of popcorn and perfume gave way to golden
rod, water lilies and wild roses. It was Uncle
Harry Doyle who broke the mood when he
remarked that he did not know "the British"
and "the Japs" had had so much in common.
"The *English*," insisted Aunt Betty MacLellan
which only set them off once again along
familiar antiquarian paths. Tales that always
led to Culloden, the Bonnie Prince, Scots
selling out the way the Irish never did;
Highland dancing just so much leaping about,
Irish neutrality and too many nights at the Legion....

While our parents divided themselves
and their time between bingo and the Steel City
Tavern, we hacked our way in dreams through
the deep Burma bush whistling that rousing
marching tune while trying to remember
the name of the token Canadian kid (champion
swimmer from Montreal) who carried crippled
Jack Hawkins but, when pressed, could not kill
in a close-up.

Sydney-Glace Bay Drive-In

We hunkered down on the floor
of our '56 Pontiac so the count
would be seven instead of nine.
We sang Johnny Horton's hit
from Smokey to Sydney Mines
and pointed out the window
at the stunted spruce, shouting
all the time: "Her guns were big
as trees." Mother laughed and
told us to sit back in those days
before seat belts. (How do you
buckle-up seven kids in the back
of a used Pontiac?) We politely cried
for her to come but she had bingo
and better things to do than watch
an old battleship go down. She'd wait,
she said, and see it sink on tv.

The Hood sank without ceremony
in a blinding flash that could have
been anything, really. Our father
cemented the silence by uttering
a single word in the dark—magazine.
Only later, when we saw the single
survivor (blown off the deck) on
Front Page Challenge, did we believe.

When my turn came to get popcorn
I stood transfixed, between cars
blinded with the steam of teenage
passion, as young sailors on the giant
and now silent screen spun steel wheels
on doors that sealed the young and grey
alive in the hull of the sinking flames.
In *The End* only the fog remained.

Halifax Report on Sydney Cancer Rates

Uncle Francis caught hot steel for forty years
while Aunt Helen strung clothes on the line
from nineteen to forty-two.
Then they removed her breasts;
first one, then, later, the other.

The cancer is caused by their lifestyle
they drink and smoke too much

She drank her tea in the shadow of coke ovens
crying only to herself for the air of Ingonish.
Later, it became the reassuring smell of jobs
and only strangers and relatives remarked
the stench of the Pier, the burning of eyes.

The cancer is caused by their lifestyle
they drink and smoke too much

Summer days in Ingonish as a girl
she gathered simple shells, stones
and sticks, bones bleached by the
endless blue. Then, 12 years on, she
chased and changed six kids in sight
of the Keltic Lodge. But the beach was
always Trinidad, Tobago and Key West
—the scent of pine and spruce in the salt
air of Middle Head.

The cancer is caused by their lifestyle
they drink and smoke too much

Despite her fuming idols of the screen
—Garbo, Bogart and Raft—she never

felt the need to join that sad generation
of smokestacks, but she always had a cold
beer for Francis smiling as he washed
down the day's dust.

The cancer is caused by their lifestyle
they drink and smoke too much

"Mastectomy" was the technical term
used by the young St. Rita's surgeon
as he explained why she couldn't survive.
My mother remembered that he never
remarried because the eldest daughter
became mother. At 67, she said, he died,
but this, she recalled, was not unexpected
of a man who worked at Sydney Steel
where they drink and smoke too much.

Down by the Tar Ponds

He's so deaf now I'm shouting all the time
we walk by where the last blast furnace died:
Must've been hell, that fire, worse than the mine?
We didn't care, we were young, full of pride

Taking a paycheque back that size, a kid,
Sixteen. You left home to work in the mines?
I hated to fish, that stinking bait, those lines.
Your father loved Ingonish, he never said
much, he was quiet, knew I'd made up my mind.
We walked on, on to the edge of the ponds.
He'd lost his wife to cancer, he'd lost friends.

Will anyone pay at all for these crimes?

He was silent, standing, as if alone,
I turned and shouted out a second time.
I'm deaf, son, not dumb, yes, we were blind.

But tell me what's the cost of staying home?

Cape Breton Journal

"Imagination is memory"
—James Joyce

I

The healing heat of mid-July
on my brother's backstep, a ghettoblaster's
    steady pulse, charcoal
and beer for prodigal sons
    turned perennial tourists.
Blue sky and old songs betray
    a sentimental refrain found
in nostalgia for Charlotte and George
    Streets in the days of rock'n roll,
the Ranch Boys, Beatles and The New Broom.
    Back when blast furnaces of the Pier
cooked New Waterford's coal
    while generous parents poured money
into the ample pockets of our steel city cousins:
    Catholic girls and boys who prayed
for Saturday nights
    so full of promise
they would never see Sunday morning.
    Our Sydney as hot as Australia's, and equally exotic
for romantic
    rural mice like ourselves up on a weekend pass
from Down North.
    Back then none of us knew
that even on our isolated island
    we bore witness to a generation
forever held hostage by a cult of youth;
    baby boomers doomed to dance
across the stage at sixty, wrinkled rolling
    stones splashed with uv rays,
sybils hanging in high definition cages

       cursed and cursing the zoom lens.
And always, always a desperate diet
       of comebacks until the bell
of a last round that sounds
       the end.
       Even our mothers and fathers
saw the stars and beauties
       of their childhood resurrected,
bought, and made over—raggedy Anns and Andys
       immortalized on the check-out counter.
Cape Breton was far from fame.
   An island known
for its desolate beauty
       and desperate industrial life.
A Celtic Sicily
       of the north,
a Scots Montserrat with coal and steel.
       Atlantic Canada's outport of progress,
a Mecca
       for vital but now buried
lives of penniless rich men and women
       from old immigrant worlds:
       Italy, Greece,
Poland, Ukraine,
       Russia, Lebanon,
Barbados.

II

Newfoundland fishermen,
       immortal as the ice off Labrador,
       are fossilized in the fo'c'sle of our imaginations.
They remain.
       Though every fish be canned, every haddock
caught, and cod but a frozen footnote in a great
       granddaughter's school reader;

while outports like Galtas and
    Pushthrough metamorphose into National
Peggy's Coves wrapped up in oilskins, sou'westers
    and yellow dories on Upper Canadian
calendars.
The industrial trawlers and draggers of Nat' Sea
    sunk forever beneath white waves.

History tells us
    that Bob Marley might have felt at home
in New Waterford's fourteen yard
    Calypso songs
      counterpoint to the cantos
of Napoli and Palermo,
    while in the Synagogue
of Whitney Pier sheltered a Polish Ghetto.
Mushrooms in the crowded coal cellars
    of their lives.

In Sydney
    the last of the coke ovens
lie dismembered.
    Their scattered bones reveal no secrets.
No truckstop will boast calendars
    of these behemoths or of the life and death
they breathed, for almost a century, into that lost
    and exotic world.

    There would always, always be only one master,
one destiny, one fate.

III

Along the Bras d'Or Lakes aboriginal
    songlines lie locked
in the Micmac hills of Wagmatcook.

       Silently, over the waters, Saint Ann,
an adopted adolescent elder, translates the
       hermetic hymns once chanted
over crooked crosses on Chapel Island.
The charcoal embers burn low
       on my brother's back step,
their red fire is reflected in the russet
       tourist sunset that casts its glow over
Westmount and Whitney Pier
       and as far away as Mira, Marion Bridge, Big Pond
and Louisbourg's Kennington Cove.

Ingonish Inshore
for Margaret Hawley

he fished for years
forty at least along the Ingonish shore
between Smokey and Middle Head
after twenty the city claimed one son
the sea two
you're foolish he said, thanking them
rising at four he told the time by Isaac's
old cut-boat clearing the gut
sore knees on the cold floor the "Our Father" softly intoned
the rest to himself
it's finished he said (the fishery)
in my own time too
who would have thought
only lobster would be common
and we too will soon be as rare as the haddock
but none listened
few cared
the Park would provide
short of stamps by April meant February and March in the
cab of the salt truck
the boys flinging sand out the back
and Marg at the window watching for the flash of amber
Mac somebody's tobacco and a suburbanite specialist
made him stand on the wharf
til the boats were out
with only a year left
politics, a late passion, sustained him
but only the sea they knew
could steel him

Antigonish Landing

in memory of R.J. MacSween, 1915-1990

> *"Our mind is full of sorrow, who will know of our grief?"*
> Song of the Bowmen of Shu
> Ezra Pound, from the Chinese of Shih-ching

He taught me never to second-guess
remembering Coady's rebuke to him
when he mistakenly praised McCarthy.

Taught me the cost of contradiction:
knowledge. Taught me to listen.
Silence surrounds the peep of the partridge.

Teach me now to listen, to hear the bird
hidden in the bush, full-fed, delicate.
A taste of fall, only in autumn.

1

He called his father Pa and remembered the old man
standing on the stair in anger and indignation—
sister Catherine quiet on the phone, hushing the death
of his son. His children whispering in the kitchen!
Remembered too, from four years of age,
a hug from grandfather Nicholson, fiddler.
Highland Scots from the pages of Grimm:
MacSweens and Nicholsons in molds of MacAskill.

No more perhaps than "What's your father's name?"
Cape Breton in a box, a handful of photos, black and white
prints curled like Vogue makins spilling precious memories
between straightened cracks of primitive developer and fix.
His father died in Toronto. Where else!
A private past lonely on a Spadina front step.

2

Nicholson Tower, named for his mother's brother,
Doc Pat. President, priest, uncle and mentor.
Father Rod MacSween? The fourth floor. A locked door.
Persistent knocking. Pretending not to be in.
Knocking again. Then the gentle and humorous voice:
"Go away I want to work." Later, in class, 100 students,
English 350: poetry and short story.
Sit up straight, take your foot down, stop coughing

Cannons to the left of me, cannons to the right.
The Lake Isle of Innisfree Comment. Wrong.
Escapist, I venture. Is that written in your book?
A fellow in the front row with long legs one rubbed
against the other—a Christening for life—the fly.
The bell rings, leaving no sound by The Windhover.

3

The decade gone and retirement to his books
and memories: Father Danny his best friend
from youth dead at 40 on the Glebe House path,
his face purple, his hands in his pockets.
Regrets. "I should have stayed in a parish"
and I "But the *Review*, your poems, your students?"
Dismissed. His only uttered pride a summer camp
built in Hay Cove for New Waterford's parish poor.

A young curate with a bucksaw and maul he struck
the posts alongside Mick MacKinnon. And on VE Day
Plummer Avenue, stood sentinel "scared to death"
with Father Raymond Campbell defending Favretto's store;
the angry crowd, Favretto crying in St. Agnes Glebe;
the fading shouts of "salami" and "Mussolini."

4

His only travel was by car, a mind of Europe "going down the road"
to brother, sisters, cousins, students, friends.
Uprooted Maritimers touching home in Mississauga,
gathered for the yearly Mass and cookout at MacKinnons.
Talk of his father and the strike of '25: brother George
recalling "The Bay," French soldiers from Quebec, a Colonel
Vanier; and sister Catherine cursing machine gun nests
in front of Father Charlie MacDonald's Church. Cape Breton Oka.

Then Catherine dead and George quick to follow.
His last trip, talk of Spain, a journey to the
ancient sites: it would be good to see the Prado,
Gaudi's Church of the Holy Family, the Roman ruins
of Sagunto; a pilgrimage to Santiago de Compostela.
Pleasant pipe dreams encouraged by cousins and friends.

5

In July of '86 a chance to touch the past again:
White Point, Cape Breton he had not seen since '38.
Outport priest and seminarian days he arrived
by boat to teach the fishermen's children to sing
the ABC's. Why White Point? His grandfather built the
church (gone now) and fishplant (gone too). "Would anyone
be left? They won't remember me. Archie a boy of 12.
I taught for two summers. What would he be...?"

Sitting in Richard MacDonald's kitchen, Sugar Loaf
rising from the sea, the Dixons descend the hill.
Archie giving a hug demanding a blessing.
Brothers, wives, children: "This is Father MacSween."
Looking out the window, Cape Breton's greatest view.
Do you remember the boy who drowned, the light dying....

6

The last days spent quiet watching osprey dive
above Sandersons' into the deep blue of Antigonish harbour.
His favorite scene, sacrilege for a Cape Breton son.
But these are highlands too: Coady, Tompkins, Nicholson
they also loved the view. Long drives after dinner to Cape
George, the lobster fishermen, all their "tackle and trim."
Then "the distinguished thing" some suffering, but humour
till the end. St. Martha's nurses laughing loud with him.

Then the funeral, the phrases "end of an era," "last
of the St. F. X. giants." Six young footballers carry the
coffin and worry about St. Mary's quick quarterback. Would
you have worried too? Rugby, golf, hockey, baseball
you played them all, legend has you could have made the minors.
Athlete, teacher, poet, priest, friend...we will remember them.

Jemseg bridge above Grand Lake
a Yangtze delta of willow,
poplar and ash along the Saint John.

Not oxen in the distance under yoke
for rice, but a bull moose making
his cross-country run.

He's in the water now, the great head
held aloft, the strong strokes ripple
the surface in a v-shaped wake.

Above, reflecting the v, mallards
and geese wing their way southwards
over the heads of great white pines.

Death of the Inshore

I

"Rum and fish in Ingonish" old Father Day's
Answer to the St. F. X. seminarians,
In Cape Breton's outport days.
Two sailings a week by the *Aspy*,
And the outport priest saying prayers
To Stella Maris, and comforting the seasick
And all others who wished
To reach North Sydney and the mines.
Fish? Not now, only a handful of cod:
Lobster of course, and if you're lucky
And connected, a doubly poached salmon,
But never, never a haddock.
Death of the offshore, death of the inshore:
These headlines will remain
Long after the fishery is gone,
When only the gulls cry and the seals bark echo
In the wash off Kelly's Mountain and Cape North.

II

Aging Sea Kings of Summerside burn up
The winter budget in the squalls of mid-June
Tail ends of hurricanes from the Gulf of Mexico.
The tail ends of dragons they take what's left
Of the lobster and crush the season to a close
On the rocks of White Point and Ingonish.
Such a storm took you, David Doyle,
Cousin and fisherman's son, outward bound
For Port-aux-Basques, and your father, Ronald,
Before you, struck by a wooden buoy
Hooked too quickly on the fast-driven hauler.

"Lost at Sea" carved on your wooden Celtic cross,
David. Your father they found strangely huddled
In the deep off Middle Head.

III

Ottawa cuts quotas for fish and for lifeboats
While two Cape Breton boys
Find the dory-like half of a beached oil drum.
In the June twilight it carries them out.
"If there had been a boat nearby!
If there had been a boat!"
A month later a ten-day search stops
As RAF Nimrods sight the single-handed sailor
Off Plymouth to the relief of the press
And the public. Halifax halts the hunt.
The Ontario sailor and his yacht,
Have conquered the crossing, once more.

IV

On PEI a returned Ontario native
And small town mayor is lost in
Surf at Cousins Beach, Park Corner.
No Nimrods hunt him down, they
Search only and always for
Single-handed sails off the Irish
Coast, Brittany and Land's End.
A handful of sad and grim-faced
Firemen followed a figure in the surf
And cradled the corpse for a
Grieving wife and town. A strong
Swimmer at 63, betrayed by the
Island undertow and the pull of the Gulf

As far off as Anticosti and
Les Iles de la Madeleine.

Far from the shores of Erie
The only sound a squelch and squeal
Of gulls crying in the far-off wash
Of lonely Cousins Beach.

from Ingonish Intervale

Clyburn Brook
               a river only in spring
its shallow summer stream
               boasts more golf balls
than trout.
               As boys we learned to fish them out.
From Franey Mountain
               the crystal cracks the Intervale
     a tiny Yangtze
     down to a delta
     where salt cattails
               bend to the tide's change,
and blue and white lobster boats
               of Doyle brothers point west
and rest like compass needles
               inside a blue-hardened glass.

Portuguese and Basque Right Whalers
               once boiled blubber on North Bay beach,
that some dark Iberian winter night
             might light the lamps of
Saint Lucia
             Isabella,
                 or hooded
                                   Torquemada.
No one now remembers these roughnecks
of the whaleroad,
               their pre-Columbian loneliness and pain.

Our colonial school readers paid no wages to
           these sailors, or to the blood and bone
               of slaughtered infant giants,
        Nor did we know that Wolfe had shelled
our shores.

Their songs and stories
            left no marks
                        upon the land.
            They vanished in the winds of Fall,
                        carried on decks
salted
            with the sum of all they saw.

Acadians exiled in their wake
and the dispossessed of Kerry, Donegal, and Skye.

            Hunter gatherers, our Irish
ancestors wintered in the Intervale's
            upper
                        reaches
                                    turning snow
                            scarlet with the blood
                            of young does,
sweet smelling fried meat
            on the stone hearth
            for the unrelenting solstice
            of that first December
                                    dark.

Skating below the bridge of childhood we
            saw only ourselves reflected in
                        the frozen stream.
            Indestructible amphibians, we jumped
clampers as high as cenotaphs and
                        slipped to our waists
in the jade soup at
                        Clyburn Brook's edge.
A quicksand
            of sorrow
                swallowed our infant cousin
                                    down

                the crusty bank
                        through April thin ice.
The casual statistic on the small stones
                and wooden crosses
a census carved by a carpenter's son
        affirming a stepfather's status
as widower
                and parent alone.

Stoic as eagles on the crags and cliffs
        they sheltered in stands of pine swaying
                        against a
                                bitter and accustomed
                                                fate.

The gentle summer waters of the stream
        are withdrawn and thin
                        so
                        low
                they need no Christopher
                        to carry a child across.
The saint's statue stuck to the dash of
                our father's '59 Pontiac my brother
washed mid-stream for Friday nights
        at the parish hall.

   And at the brook's mouth, below the 16th tee
the snailed spired Catholic Church pokes out
        above the Irish peasants' mounds of stone
long since carpeted for middle-class play.

Cabot Day

"John Cabot landed here in 1497."—School Reader

Cabot Day we climbed
Mount Sugar Loaf
The white cross
Gleaming in the sun
Confirming John's first one
We ran down tripping and
Yelling and Mary MacDonald
Young then shouting "Boys, boys
Go down slowly" the sun burning
The backs of our necks brought
Green shoots through the dead
Grass of early June on the mountain
But below by the shore violets and
Mayflowers around the brown picnic
Tables with the teachers talking
And laughing in their innocence again
With the children they boarded the
Buses leaving behind the freshly
Painted sign of the man who gave
Us this day in the sun.

Quebec North of Englishtown

At thirty-five the monthly call to home
always brings unwelcomed news
from childhood and from youth:
his old teacher has died.
74, a stroke, welcomed release.
"You used to date her daughter, son?
She came from Quebec? The Gaspé was it?"
Sainte Claire, their only contact with Quebec
outside Champlain, Cartier and the Habs.
Montreal was his father's team
and his by birth and accident:
child caretaker he guided Mrs. Molson
through the half-finished hotel
(the Park owns it now) and his reward
would make him hero for a week
in late winter approaching play-offs.
Two hockey sticks—Jean Belliveau and Dick Duff:
taped, signed and used. The gods had come to earth.
Not even Elvis could compete with this.
His basement became a shrine
where sticks were touched (carefully)
the signatures verified, the height debated
(Duff is taller than that)
and the wonder concluded with converts to the Habs.

"Les Canadiens" she said with elegance and with ease.
They loved to have her substitute
she could be bullied with ease.
The school often brutal with boys of 16
doing time in grade seven
Boys who one day set fire to the playground
shrubs and ripped out the live electric wire.
This he remembered from 13.

Remembered too Mrs. Doucet reading Hugo,
Les Miserables and an Australian story
about the outback called "Walkabout"
(He'd later, much later, seen the film)
Sometimes she went home to Quebec.
A pilgrimage one summer with her mother
to Sainte Anne de Beaupré.
"She was too good for this place, son."
his father said listening dark to dark
for the son's reply. "Too good," he said.

Long Distance: coast to coast

The phone had rung while she was hanging shirts
(the new dryer still a dusty Christmas gift)
Joan? she died at the scene, the daughter was unhurt.
Asleep at the wheel, a nurse at the end of her shift.

She went west with David, a burned-out Cape Breton son.
Mary, the mother, retired, left before credits were known
Joan cursed old Joseph, his wood, work and gun.
All those children no plumbing, no car, no help, no phone.

From coast to coast from C.B. to B.C.
from nurse to niece Joan laughed across the line
Get on with it, girl, Jesus, leave, let them be.
You're fifty, Martha, you're running out of time!

Life ends with death, that's it, she always said.
She shocked the nuns and uncles with her talk
He's drunk, the slob, at the Legion, he can't walk
Mother shook her head, smiled, then silently broke bread.

Calgary Breton Blues

They say that it's a very nice town now
(the plant is closed, the tar ponds quite far off.)
Mother says: it's a steal for 70 thou.
Though the neighbours are loud, poor and rough.
It's not their fault that they're the way they are.
It's MacEachen's legacy, his grants, handouts, and beer.

Tell Bill there is a rink in every town,
we saw it when we drove the Cabot Trail
Westerners are right to curse and frown,
Big Allan and his kind should be in jail.
The food's o.k. although I hate the cod.
They love it here, it seems very close, or next, to God.

Most of all I miss West Edmonton, those boutiques.
There's nothing here at all, but Zellers, Sears
Of course it's old junk they couldn't sell, shipped east.
And yes, stupid Larry loves the hockey, talk, jokes and beer!

Knight Inlet, B.C.

A man with one leg and a hard hat
Stared at the ground while the white letters
Of the poster proclaimed to the loggers
How to lose thirty pounds in thirty seconds.

The jade water, humpback salmon and a
Nine-foot grizzly with a patch on his back
(Who tolerated black bears in the dump)
Kept us company through the short hours

On long days like Sundays we watched struggling
Salmon complete the journey of sun and stars
Dying and rotting in the rivulets ignored by the
Bears and useful to no one but part of the process

The loggers too struggled and staggered
With sixty-pound blocks on their backs
I always imagined them Bunyan-like, red-checkered
And shod with hobnailed boots but

On arrival only the boots looked familiar
Worn by elf-like men in green and brown
From the unromantic Maritimes: pulp cutters from
Pictou County and boys from New Brunswick

Even a cousin from Cape Breton who,
"Second loading" one wet Saturday,
Watched a cedar crush his legs
And hopes for a farm in Iona

Indians from Salmon-Arm and Spuzzum
Laughed and joked in the cab of the "Crummy"

They seemed contented though not promoted
To the whiteman's club of "Riggin' slingers"

Only once, when whisky arrived,
Did the words buck and bastard
Rise to the surface in the
"Last floating camp on the coast"

Quick money redeemed the time, or so we believed
Pipe-dreaming our way in pubs and taverns in
Burnaby, Penticton and Banff; one or two saved
And survived but the rest returned to begin
Again their last season of struggle on the shore.

Homemade Stars
for Frances MacDonald, R.N.

You used needlepoint at the end of every shift
to put all those night blues into a tired nativity scene.
   Your shipmates on Four North West admired Mary
half-dressed in August heat: a madonna sitting astride
an astonished donkey who seemed uncertain about his
ears, or at least about what he'd overheard. Joseph had
no head, only the outline of a hat, at which an old nurse
remarked "you might want to leave him like that."

Frayed cloth from Fabricville holds willing captives,
as each point of acupuncture drugs a raw nerve.
   Some nights, you admit, are harder than others:
heavy old women and frail male drunks who swing
blind in the dark, sybils who seldom miss their mark.
(Five stars and a crescent moon halo for Jesus) These
calls are accepted in silence with sore wrists and sciatic
strain. No, it's "head cases" (physical not mental) who
slow the night passage. Young men battered on New
Brunswick's roads. All the male pain of seventeen
in a straw spit in anguish among the confused traffic
of a polished floor.

Jesus is finished now, and Joseph has his haloed head in record
time—a hurried up offence to flee this night's abuse.
   A forefinger and thumb escape to Egypt, far away from
Herod, his army, and GM, its cars full of angry young men.

Partridge Island, Saint John

for Danny Britt

Loyalist mothers sang Barbara Allan and
old English lullabies to their seasick
children in holds of three-masters anchored
on high Fundy tides. Uprooted New Yorkers

and Connecticut Yankees clearing pine and
spruce from the water's edge. America's
Atlantic Exodus. There were trees on the island
then, just as there must have been the plump

and delicate Partridge of birch and spruce.
But 60 years would pass before this small
harbour rock acquired permanent wood again,
roots from Donegal to Cork, from Maine to Newark.

A Saint John name forever linked by pain
to poor Irish passage in the holds of timber
ships. A tiny Ethiopian Emerald Isle, a village
from typhonic Bangladesh or a Peruvian

Andes town. In the cold footnotes of history
cholera, typhus, timber, children and coffin-
ships are analyzed and understood as products
of a laissez-faire. But the Slave Ship of Turner

returns the bold stare of truth: the boiling sea
corrodes the gain of goods. In 1847 eight
hundred and twenty-three burials at sea from
Cork to the Nova Scotia coast. On the island in

June mist, sheds house the fever from ships
and town. They've never seen anything like this.

A Saint John son answers the city's call for care,
and the young intern rows out in the fine rain.

Rows out to confront the rumour and pain.
He will be home soon, but again he asks his
merchant father to comfort his young bride:
"Please see to Mary for me, she worries so."

The old man shakes the hand of his young
doctor son, but James Patrick Collins,
M.D. at twenty-three, would not see
the summer's end or birth of Elizabeth Catherine.

Only a coffin sealed in lead could land on
the city's shore. Thousands followed the
file of priests. A hero, one of their own,
someone who gave the crossing worth,

a boy trained by London and Paris, an
Irishman who made it work. A widowed
Mary Collins, Mary Quinn of Mooncoin,
worked for the poorhouse and sang

Irish lullabies to daughter "Isabella."
This is the fine print behind the Saint John
Celtic crosses. History questions the island's
worth. Its place amid the facts: thousands

died at Grosse Isle, Quebec; the young
doctor needed money; New Brunswick
Irish were prosperous and pre-Famine.
A sentimental love of Hard Times?

Bounderby up by his bootstraps. So
the rhetoric of schoolroom and street.

A modern crossroad where legend and
myth, religion and need must privately

meet, or not at all. The port misses container
traffic now as Halifax hordes and bosses;
our Maritime Toronto. Scattered pulp boats
and Irving tankers leave lonely plumes of

smoke on the Fundy's edge, while out on the
island a new beacon sends its steady beam
of broken intervals far past Red Head
and the wake of Digby ferry's lights.

General James Wolfe enroute from Halifax to Quebec, 1759

Louisbourg lies east, he left it last July
a heap of smouldering boundary stones;
    six weeks to breach Vauban's walls;
now it is June again and the cliffs of Quebec
    await him.
He is anxious to fight, but finds it hard
to win fame. Montcalm has good ground,
    but time stops with Wolfe.
Last year he burned a fishing village
out there on Isle Royale's eastern shore,
    Ingonish by the chart.
The cliffs fell to the sea as at Dover and Donegal.
No casualties, no prisoners, the smoke of his
    cannons scattered all into the dark
and virgin Micmac demesne.
    On the Miramichi they did the same.
Cape Breton has lost its pride of place.
It has much rugged beauty but boasts only fish
    and coal.
His pardoned Culloden Scots prisoners will remember
these shores, will return
    to these lordless highlands.
Their cause is dead.
    The king over the water will come no more.
But all have sworn to fight for Wolfe.
In Halifax he sent salt cod back home to his
    mother and father.
He reads Gray late into the night, and picks
    a popular elegy off Englishtown to calm
his officers below the Plains of Abraham.

Loyalists Landing at Sydney

after Lewis Parker's painting

Boat people landing in the snow,
two men pulling a sled over stumps.
    It is November 1784
They have good woollens but none
    wear gloves.
The ground is frozen.
    A north easter funnels down
the harbour lifting a minister's cloak
    above his bare calves.
He reads his Bible above the blazing fire
    while a woman boils potatoes
and salt cod. A man, under a spared elm
    tree, lifts his head to the word
of the Lord God.
    A mother, cradling her infant,
stands frozen like Lot's wife looking back
    at all she has lost:
a swing her father made, rose bushes,
    magnolias, the Sunday walk along
the Common, the cries and calls of a market,
her second-born son under Zion Hill.

In the Martello Tower of Saint John
a Texas tourist wonders why they left.
    My brother, the guide, gives out
the facts of history, the National Park
    heritage tour. The unsatisfied
patriot nods his head unconvinced.
    Irish Scots Cape Bretoners we
connive with those
    Loyalist ancestors and fire
a parting salvo at Atlanta:
    "How 'bout those Jays!"

Later in O'Leary's pub we debate,
    over bitter bottled Guinness,
the Loyalist legacy.
    Imperial overdogs seeking
the status quo? or hardened Scots
    Presbyterians fleeing another
Culloden? When the drinks have run
    low the local bartender confesses
he never knew there were Loyalists
in Sydney, "at least not like here."

In Lew Parker's painting there is no hint
of highland clearances, of steel workers,
    Jewish or Lebanese pedlars,
the life of Whitney Pier.
    The long boats forever unload
immigrants on the shore. After this exodus
there will be no more.

The White Buildings on Shea's Hill
for Ann MacLellan Donovan

1

They're gone now, the old schools.
    Expelled for being early.
They had been left in detention for ten years,
    And they looked tired: their foundations,
Needing costly care, crumbled;
    Their floors were on the verge of collapse;
Those windows, sirens of broken daydreams,
    Were long since shattered.
In the end, they failed to make the grade—
    Knocked down one afternoon in June
For want of imagination.

    For forty years or more they had looked
Out over Ingonish from Smokey Mountain
    To Middle Head. Our generation was
Pre-Vatican II and post-Elvis:
    In schoolboard terms, the shoe was full.
Sister Athanasius' Primary class spilled over
    Shea's Hill with hurrying laughter and small
Feet, sounds that echoed as far away as the Whitty
    Shore and the narrow Creek, our Peggy's Cove,
Where all the village waters meet.

The hill was so steep we were hunched over
    Like old men and women, at five and six.
Our oversized heads down, from a distance
    We could have been office workers or
Peruvian Indians filing up an Andes mountain trail.
    Our llamas all gone lame and only enough food
To last until recess, but plenty of stationary supplies,

  Including our lovely long pencils
Which we could not wait to sharpen, even though
  We knew they couldn't be held between forefinger
And thumb—as snug as Paladin's derringer gun.

  Our hearts were broken, for the morning at least,
When Sister Athanasius snapped those elegant orange
  HB's in three, and placed the remains in a collective box.
Our first political experience: "there must be pencils for all."
  Then the sandbox at recess, a joy from November
Until marble days, but demanding civility, a sharing
  Of corners, manners, and the concept of linear time.
The ABC's also ran round in a line at the top of the room:
  Cards in green and white with capitals and lower case.
A sister of St. Martha, we prayed at the end of every day
  For Father Buddy, our buddy, (her brother?)
And the people of his parish in Santo Domingo.
  Haiti's silent Spanish cousin.

Mary MacDonald looked like Jackie Kennedy
  Long before the Jackie Kennedy look.
Although the time was right,
  In our memories her year faded
Like all those early tv shows that weren't cartoons.
  She had to settle for second place
Even though she taught First Grade.
  Her husband, the Park warden, was called Dan R
To distinguish him from all those other MacDonalds.
  He died young in our years,
It was Grade Five when we squeezed
  Into narrow pews to hear High Mass.
Grade One was a rite of passage, finishing school for primary.
  Once over, we left that two-room home forever,
Our only contact from Grade Two the marbles we pitched
  Under its steps. Graduating down those high stairs
For the last time, stairs that gave a great view of the harbour,

But would still have disturbed Maria Montessori
Even though small signs of her care (the doorknobs were low)
    Were visibly there.

2

We had not seen Sister Athanasius since primary,
    And her dark form in the door told us something
Was wrong. "Are there any Donovan children here?"
    Crying free of her hug he scrambled for the stairs
At the word fire and saw the smoke too clearly
    Through the scalding eyes.
Earlier, he'd felt a similar fear as the Cuban missile
    Crisis drew near; it crossed through the arm
Of his mother's chair courtesy of Coca-Cola and CBC.
    Remembered, too, Mary Cooke crying in mid-afternoon
Because of a city the class thought was close,
    But Dallas was down in Texas;
Even so, she let all her Grade Fours go.

    In Grade Five our post-colonial geographies
Took us to Malaysia with a pygmy boy called Bunga?
    Who travelled with his hunter-gatherer father
In Sabah? or Sarawak? along the alluvial coastal plain.
    They seemed forever on the run down that hot,
Humid finger of land that looked like Florida but stopped
    Short of Singapore—Malaysia's Miami.
Tin, Portuguese and iron ore, British and Buddhists
    All got honorable mention. But Islam, rubber and oil
(petroleum products) held pride of place, seemed to cover
    The map. Squatting on their small feet,
Neither the pygmies nor the Grade Five class
    Could foresee where the highways would meet.

Sister Winnifred, as tough as Eddie Shack,
    The last nun the class would know in white and black.

That summer before Grade Six gave hints of puberty
    And the cost of pleasure and anarchy to come—
Our class would soon be on the run. Grade Seven
    Was still a myth in the mind of Grade Six.
The last room in the old school, it had held forever baby
    Bonus adults: boys ducktailed with Elvis cuts
Who drove Chevys and pick-ups; girls who looked
    Like Miss Kitty in *Gunsmoke*, and who waved
Export A—the toughest fag—in fingers tipped with red spears.
    They were all too young for their years,
Including Sister Winnifred who battled and lost an unknown
    Woman's disease our government later called cancer.

The foundations have been filled now,
    You can park your car in Grade Seven
And see the Keltic Lodge and Freshwater Lake
    Where the school used to skate on sunny weekday
Afternoons—if Mars was in line with the Seven Sisters
    So the principal's mood was right. The parish hall,
Burned and rebuilt, looks like a bunker from *The Guns of Navarone*,
    While the old high school has reverted to childhood,
And elementary instruction.

    The memories are palpable here—on top of Shea's Hill—
The small shadows forever playing "pitch you last," tag
    And hopscotch. What they unknowingly ask us is not much—
Although it can cost everything—they demand not to be
    Made better, but simply not to be denied.

A Japanese Western

When I told my grandfather
The Magnificent Seven was Japanese
he said I should have my head examined.
It was as if I'd said Hank Snow was Hungarian
(which maybe he is).
Years later, while watching a dubbed version
of Kurosawa's *Ran,* I told him it was based
on Shakespeare's *King Lear*
"It figures," was all he said.

Bewley's Oriental Café, Dublin

Red hair and freckles he looked so much
like brother Glen I asked him for a match:
"American," he said. "No, Canadian," I pleaded.
After three weeks someone felt at ease
enough to ask what the difference was.
Not much, in fact, I explained
but added that in feeling
it would come close to calling
him Scots or Welsh.
"Not English," he asked
No, not English.

He wanted to know why we persecuted Quebec
(He had read Brian Moore's little book)
"They're Catholics like us," he said.
"No, not like you, and things are different,
it's not like the North." I defended.
"And the Queen," he smiled.
Silenced, I spoke of Hollywood, last outposts,
Sudbury, Kingston, of Toronto's Italians and Indians.
No, not Natives.

Tim Horton's patrons would have second cups
in Bewley's Oriental Café. Their sticky buns
and cakes may be more exotic, but Karsh's
photograph of Beckett always brings old
Ambrose Whitty back to mind
and to mend too the fishnets for the cold Irish waters
off Ingonish, Cape Breton.

Dublin's McLuhan

in memoriam

The BBC beamed his image
into a Baggot Street pub
producing mild interest in
the message, then a channel
change to rugby (Scotland and Wales)
he would have approved, smiled,
enjoyed the game

I only heard him once (live)
in Ottawa a pro-life protest
he joked, then spoke of Sputnik
creating our village
few listened, fewer understood
(*Finnegans Wake* a song?
and Bloom what a flower does)
but those that heard applauded

He was McLuhan, his subject did not matter
Muggeridge followed without probes
in the language of the Mass
misunderstood in Dublin
your star rose and fell until
in Leeson Street (Marist Chapel)
another Mass gathered a faithful
few who knelt and felt they knew
the message of this man

dead 3 thousand miles away in Canada
1 minute from everywhere

Liscomb Sanctuary

in memory of the 26 coal miners
who died at Plymouth, Nova Scotia

A New Glasgow honeymoon couple
kisses for one night only in the luxury
of Liscomb Lodge: here, on Nova Scotia's
Eastern shore, a lonely lighthouse can still
signal codes for late lobster fishermen and
perhaps, too, for the few remaining trawlers
bound with quotas cut for Canso. But rumour
has it that in three weeks only the stars of Asia
Minor will flash for lovers on this coast still
intent on romantic lights.

As a girl, four years back, the young bride,
Sally Doucette, baby-sat bored brothers and
sisters who possessed the natural contempt
for history as they ran, cried and begged to
leave Historic Sherbrooke Village. They don't
care if it's good for them, and only once did
their dark eyes bulge bright and wide with
wonder: "A forge, a forge," cried the bride
in dictionary definition through the roar of
the tiny blast furnace cooking lobster-
red shoes for the great brown Belgians that
steamed and stamped in the dark lonely stalls.

Bored, uninformed, Sally too longed to be back
home, back and busy at McDonald's on the East
River Road where romance, gentle gossip and
Madonna echoed between the stainless steel
fryers on Saturday nights. And where quiet John
MacLellan always ordered the Big Mac special
until Sally gently bullied him to change. Doing
so she won the boast and the five-dollar bet

placed back in the kitchen where the chorus of
co-workers had continually cried it couldn't be done.

Today the honeymooners camp at Ecum Secum
on their return journey from five nights in Dartmouth.
They visit the village now as young adults
and wonder at "so much to see" the strange silence
of absent comforts: cars, radios and tvs. "It's quiet
like Louisbourg," Sally says. John's father had helped
build the fortress, a laid-off Cape Breton coal miner
he resurrected stones blown away by Lord Byron's
grandfather to keep the French forever from
Nova Scotia's coast. John MacLellan, the miner's son,
had only once been underground, and would not go
again because good luck and a friend's bad back at
François Michelin's Trenton plant had saved him
from the Ford seam, or the long nights on the new
dole line of Oshawa.

When the news of the twenty-six came,
they wanted the day postponed, but
family and friends counselled with
comforting clichés, old stoic Scots' sayings
about life not working that way. Now,
in the silence of Sherbrooke Village, John
recalls his father's words from the wedding
afternoon, sitting out back on Doucette's
freshly painted porch, while fiddlers and
dancers from Sydney Mines compete with
a reel from within: "In the old days politicians
knew how far they could push, knew too
there was a line they dare not cross."

Ten miles away in Liscomb
Game Sanctuary the deer
do not know they are safe.

They walk carefully on their
coal black feet, alert to all
things under the stars.
They do not know that the
old dispensation is dead,
so they will not rest in the
still comfort of these crooked
and abandoned fields.

Cape Breton Christmas

Brueghel might have seen a reason for
    living in a village like this, with
three small lobster boats buried to the stems;
and only old MacDougall knows
    that the "Ricky and Randy" rots inside
its snow shell.

In the village, wood fires in evening
    light reclaim traditional places
smoking slowly in twenty below blue from newly cleaned
chimneys; snow-covered cords of neatly stacked birch and spruce
    steal attention from the hibernating rows
of lobster traps.

On the roofs crows and ravens wait
    for Mary MacDougall's white arm bearing a red bowl
of bread crusts, bacon rinds and dried gingercake
flung far from the steps for crow, raven and gull
    cursed as scavengers. Only the jay
braves the broom to feed on the back porch.

In the Christmas Eve quiet of the vestry
    the newly appointed parish priest
stacks hockey sticks and rolls of tape; Sister
Arsenault smiles at the thought of the eyes of
    the prayer-book receiving boys.

It is now two days since sun and rain flooded
    the forest with silver thaw; no longer naked
the bent birch splits crystal light through
rainbow branches. But Leo Doyle on Christmas call
    knows the reach of silver trees: cracked insulators
and inch-thick ice on the line.

Suppertime brings cold-toed Whitty children home
    to cocoa and brown beans, leaving only
old MacDougall on the ice; he has two dozen now,
smelting since three under his freshly cut fir: one smelt
    every ten minutes entices but his toes too
tell the time.

Five village lamps compete with stars
    as the Doyle children refuse the rides
of their midnight neighbours. Set in snow-covered
spruces the gothic structure echoes with whispers
    at the back where handshakes
jam the doors.

Up front Saint Patrick's statue, returned
    from dust and banishment, glows green
in the Christmas lights of the new-cut crib.
On the granite slopes of Smokey
    Leo Doyle unhooks his spurs
as freckled boys shout

"Hockey sticks!" and kitchen lights burn late
    for sleepy mothers with final touches to
turkeys and toys. CBC presents the Queen in
white on channel two (the working one)
    and an unignored storm warning:
at Philip's Nose

the mountain will cut the village off
    (for the night at least) but the storm-stayed
children dream through drifts of forty feet, while
Leo Doyle gets overtime and not so lowly satisfaction
    from the now familiar flash
of the truck's revolving amber light.

Post War Mementos

I

When our father returned from overseas
he spent six weeks on the porch couch
fighting dreams laden with red berries.
Friendly fire was stillborn in those days
as the hawthorn hedge turned lethal
and shook to the sound of sten guns:
"Why do you think they're hopping!"
Young fool of a corporal (same age
as yourself) came all the way from
Nova Scotia, but wouldn't stop until
that suburban shrub of Holland brushed
him like hemlock. "It didn't look like sleep
when I crawled past him, not even at night."

II

Cologne was no longer covered with fire
or light, so you could still see the stars and
steeples of childhood. But St. Brigid could
not be found among Benedictine monks,
and the big dipper hangs on heavier nails;
here, galvanized steel spikes hold fast the
ancient plough of your peasant ancestors.
Farmers and fishermen, they were always
reluctant warriors, especially when
press-ganged by English sailors to populate
newly conquered Acadia. They deserted
Louisbourg for the galtees and glens of new
world Hebrides in the highlands of Cape
Breton. Now they sleep forever in village

Ingonish where, like scattered fish meal,
they seep into the parish loam of legend.

III

Far from thoughts of them in the spring
of '45, our father toured the Strassen
of the ruined city. Remembering his uncle
Mike, a Cape Breton mick who went
over the top in '16 with "idiot orangemen"
from Ontario. Boys who believed in Empire
but carried no Kipling or Oxford Book of
English Verse in their khaki school satchels.
It was simply a chance at romance for most,
and paid for work for Maritimers in those
days before the dole. Most of these history
lessons Mick Doyle conceded. And he laughed
at the idea of home as a place back west.

IV

In those first weeks after the fall
Cologne's children might rattle tin
drums or obey a code of condemned
youth. "You can still be shot in the street,"
his older brother Isadore believed as they
walked across to the British mess.
A tank gunner, he had fought up the Italian
coast, but would soon be demobbed.
Sooner than our father, who told his brother
about a way to get back home.
"I've joined up for Japan," he grinned and
Isadore told him he was crazy. His commander
said so too and recommended psychiatric

evaluation. "It's a hell of a way to get back
east," was all the doctor declared, admiring
the common sense nostalgia behind the lines.
You both knew that three weeks leave might
end the war. And what Mountie worth his rations
would hunt a local boy from raw German towns
in the summer woods of those native Highlands?

V

Rural children of the 60's we caddied
for those early Americans who followed
in the footsteps of Graham Bell and hiked
through the Highlands National Park.
Poor cousins of fame, they came to relax
in our fledgling tourist village. "This man
had been Elizabeth Taylor's doctor, that
one..." and so rumour followed rumour in
the kitchens of our working-class lives.
Later, my brother in curiosity confirmed
the existence of one of these faded figures
from our past: "Dr. Kelly worked with
Oppenheimer at Los Alamos." He was
always old because he shuffled along
the back eight holes with arthritic knees.
He had to run down hills in short quick
steps to keep from falling down. After
hitting the ball, he picked delicate
mushrooms, breaking their stems and
placing the brown-bottomed gills softy in
the ample pockets of his khaki windbreaker.
Once filled, he refused to play anymore.

VI

In the postwar classrooms of St. F. X.
Cape Breton boys studied philosophy
on DVA grants. In those years too some
G.I. Bill Catholics from New England still
defended the flight of the Enola Gay, even
though the young professor priest quietly
insisted "they were non-combatants." In
Ingonish our father spent that August leave
of '45 pulling his grandfather's salmon net.
The early morning mist on Franey mountain
brought back memories of black forests long
since deserted by bear and deer. Below, on
the silent and abandoned beach, the boy veteran
chased our mother under the great white clouds
that hung between the pine and spruce cliffs
of Smokey and Middle Head.

ALSO AVAILABLE FROM
Breton Books & Music

SILENT OBSERVER
written & illustrated
by CHRISTY MacKINNON
A children's book of emotional and historical substance—the autobiographical story of a little girl who lived both in rural Cape Breton and in the world of a deaf person.
$21.50

WATCHMAN AGAINST THE WORLD
by FLORA McPHERSON
The Remarkable Journey of Norman McLeod and his People from Scotland to Cape Breton Island to New Zealand
A detailed picture of the tyranny and tenderness with which an absolute leader won, held and developed a community—and a story of the desperation, vigour, and devotion of which the 19th-century Scottish exiles were capable.
$16.25

CASTAWAY ON CAPE BRETON
Two Great Shipwreck Narratives in One Great Book!
1. Ensign Prenties' *Narrative* of Shipwreck at Margaree Harbour, 1780 (Edited with an Historical Setting and Notes by G. G. Campbell)
2. Samuel Burrows' *Narrative* of Shipwreck on the Cheticamp Coast, 1823 (With Notes on Acadians Who Cared for the Survivors by Charles D. Roach)
$13.00

CAPE BRETON BOOK OF THE NIGHT
Stories of Tenderness & Terror
51 extraordinary, often chilling, tales, pervaded with a characteristic Cape Breton tenderness—a tough, caring presentation of experience
$16.25

ARCHIE NEIL
by MARY ANNE DUCHARME
From the Life & Stories of Archie Neil Chisholm of Margaree Forks, C. B.
Saddled with polio, pride, and a lack of discipline, Archie Neil lived out the contradictory life of a terrific teacher floundering in alcoholism. This extraordinary book melds oral history, biography and anthology into "the triumph of a life."
$18.50

THE MOONLIGHT SKATER
by BEATRICE MacNEIL
9 Cape Breton Stories & The Dream
From a mischievous blend of Scottish & Acadian roots, these stories blossom, or explode softly, in your life. Plus her classic play set in rural Cape Breton.
$11.00

DOWN NORTH:
The Original Book of
Cape Breton's Magazine
Word-and-Photo Portrait from the first 5 years of *Cape Breton's Magazine*
239 pages, 286 photographs
$23.50

CAPE BRETON LIVES:
A Second Book from
Cape Breton's Magazine
300 pages of Life Stories • 120 photos
$23.50

HIGHLAND SETTLER
by CHARLES W. DUNN
A Portrait of the Scottish Gael in Cape Breton and Eastern Nova Scotia
"This is one of the best books yet written on the culture of the Gaels of Cape Breton and one of the few good studies of a folk-culture."—*Western Folklore*
$16.25

• PRICES INCLUDE GST & POSTAGE IN CANADA •

CONTINUED ON NEXT PAGE

ALSO AVAILABLE FROM
Breton Books & Music

STERLING SILVER
by SILVER DONALD CAMERON
Rants, Raves and Revelations
Essays from over 25 years, never before in book form—*Sterling Silver* is a kind of autobiography of the life and interests of Silver Donald. From suicide to love and fear, craftsmanship and community—this is Silver Donald Cameron angry, hopeful, incisive and amused.
$21.50

CAPE BRETON CAPTAIN
by Captain DAVID A. McLEOD
Reminiscences from
50 Years Afloat & Ashore
A rough-and-tumble autobiography of sailing, shipwreck, mutiny, and love.
$16.25

ECHOES FROM LABOR'S WARS
by DAWN FRASER
Industrial Cape Breton in the 1920s
Echoes of World War One
Autobiography & Other Writings
Dawn Fraser's narrative verse and stories are a powerful, compelling testament to courage, peace & community.
They belong in every home,
in every school.
$13.00

A FOLK TALE JOURNEY THROUGH THE MARITIMES
by HELEN CREIGHTON
eds. Michael Taft & Ronald Caplan
72 folk tales from a lifetime of collecting. Dr. Creighton introduces each storyteller, and then lets them talk to us directly, in their own words. A wonderful portrait of the faith and courage of the collector and the trust of the storyteller.
This book is a Maritime treasure.
$23.50

THE CAPE BRETON GIANT
by JAMES D. GILLIS
& "Memoir of Gillis" by Thomas Raddall
"Informative, entertaining, outrageous...!"
$10.00

THE SPECIALINK BOOK
by SHARON HOPE IRWIN
with chapters by Linda Till, Karen Vander Ven, Dale Borman Fink
SpeciaLink is a national network based in Cape Breton devoted to getting *all* children with special needs into mainstream childcare—the real world, rather than segregated settings. This is the story of the road to these principles, and of the symposium that made them the national agenda.
$18.50

• PRICES INCLUDE GST & POSTAGE IN CANADA •

ALSO AVAILABLE FROM
Breton Books & Music
• Plus: CAPE BRETON MUSIC ON CASSETTE & COMPACT DISC •

Johnny Wilmot: ANOTHER SIDE OF CAPE BRETON

Joyous Cape Breton muic—the best studio recordings of fiddler Johnny Wilmot and friends. These extraordinary examples of Cape Breton fiddle tradition are rooted in the house parties and dances of the Northside. Driving, emotional, and absolutely unbeatable!

CD: $23.50 • Cassette Tape: $15.25

CAPE BRETON FIDDLERS ON EARLY LPS
Dan R. MacDonald • Theresa MacLellan
Dan Joe MacInnis • Donald MacLellan
Johnny Wilmot

Five great Cape Breton violinists, and their accompanists—from the masters of unavailable LP records from the 1940s & '50s. Great introduction to Cape Breton music!

Cassette Tape: $15.25

Winston "Scotty" Fitzgerald: CLASSIC CUTS

The impeccable fiddling of Winston "Scotty" Fitzgerald created the classic—the modern Cape Breton style. These 49 tunes have been digitally remastered—Winston never sounded better!

CD: $23.50 • Cassette Tape: $15.25

Winston "Scotty" Fitzgerald: HOUSE PARTIES & 78S

All the unavailable 78 rpm records with Winston on fiddle, Beattie Wallace, piano, and Estwood Davidson, guitar; plus Winston's choice of his party tapes—90 minutes

Cassette Tape: $15.25

MIKE MACDOUGALL'S TAPE FOR FR. HECTOR

Ingonish's beloved fiddler—exciting one-hr. cassette, great for listening or dancing.

Cassette Tape: $15.25

• PRICES INCLUDE GST & POSTAGE IN CANADA •

Breton Books & Music
Wreck Cove, Cape Breton Island, Nova Scotia
B0C 1H0

Cape Breton Quarry
*is set in Adobe Garamond typeface
and printed at* **City Printers** *in Sydney,
Cape Breton Island for* **Breton Books**